MONEY

Now you have it. Now you don't

Written and compiled by Kathleen Russell and Larry Wall

Published by
Walrus Productions

Published by Walrus Productions
4805 NE 106th St. Seattle, WA 98125

Text layout and typography by Ronald M. Russell

Printed by Vaughan Printing, Nashville, Tennessee

MONEY
Now you have it. Now you don't.
Kathleen Russell & Larry Wall
p. cm.
ISBN 0-9635176-4-3
   1. Quotations, English. 2. American wit and humor. 3. Wealth --
Humor.   I. Russell, Kathleen F., 1950- II. Wall, Larry C., 1949-

Printed in the United States of America

10 9 8 7 6 5 4 3 2

INTRODUCTION

We have assembled this unique collection of selected whimsical words of wisdom in the hope that others will share the inspiration, humor and reflections they have given to us.

ACKNOWLEDGMENTS

We are both deeply grateful to Ronald Russell for his generous time, dedication, encouragement and suggestions. It has been a very enjoyable and fine learning experience working with him.

We also wish to thank Steve and Margie Norman, Michelle Stringer, Roman Lemeshkov and Mark Gilman for being the friendly and honest sounding board we needed.

It all comes down to dollars and no sense.

Don't look for
the return on the money
but
the return *of* the money.

Never invest in anything that eats, sleeps or needs repairing!

Sometimes the money you
save doing it yourself
may come in handy for
getting it done over !

Those who condemn wealth
are often those
who have nothing and see
little chance of getting it.

They say money talks
but all mine says is
good-bye.

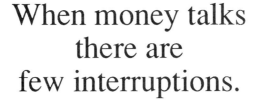

When money talks there are few interruptions.

When big bucks
are up for grabs
there are no such things
as friends.

When money speaks, the truth keeps silent.

The best place
to find a helping hand
is at the end of your arm.

Whoever says that money
doesn't buy happiness
just doesn't know
where to shop !

He who gathers firewood warms himself twice.

One must choose between
making money
and spending it;
there is no time for both.

The brain is wonderful.
It starts the moment
you get up in the morning
and does not stop until
you get to the office.

People who wake up and find success haven't been asleep.

Make money your god and it will plague you like the devil.

Money is the Christmas gift
everyone in the family wants
trouble is,
you can't charge it !

Just about the time
you make both ends meet,
somebody moves the ends.

The high cost of living
isn't so bad if
you don't have to
pay for it.

When everybody has money
they cut taxes
and when we're broke
they raise them !

It takes more brains to
fill out an income tax form
than to make the income.

The IRS has finally put poverty within our reach.

America is a land of
untold wealth
most of it untold
around April 15th.

The mind is like the stomach
it's not how much
you put into it that counts,
but how much it digests.

Nowadays, if somebody
pays cash,
you have to wonder
if their credit is any good.

Don't worry
if you borrow
only if you lend.

Creditors
have better memories than
debtors.

It is not what you can
afford to have
but what you can
afford to lose.

Nothing grows faster
than the unpaid balance on a
revolving charge account.

The more you need a loan the harder it is to get one.

Nobody ever went broke
saving money.

Checkbook errors invariably result in a lower balance.

Don't put your trust
in money, but
put your money
in trust.

Simplified tax form:
How much money did you
make last year? $_____
Send it in.

There is no such thing as enough money.

I have enough money
to last the rest of my life
...*unless* I buy something.

There are those
who gain from their wealth
only the fear of losing it.

Make money the old fashioned way... marry into it or inherit it !

Sometimes the worst thing
about
owning your own business
is the boss.

Money is like manure...
spread it around and
it does good,
pile it up and it stinks.

The nicest thing about money
is that it never clashes
with what you wear.

Wealth can't buy health, but health can buy wealth.

Wealth is a result of habit.

Remember, you are rich
according to what you are
not according to
what you have.

He is rich
who has enough to be
charitable.

When it comes to giving,
some people stop at
nothing.

Money won't buy happiness
but it will pay for
a research staff to
study the question.

Poverty is no disgrace
it's just so
confoundedly inconvenient.

Nobody ever drowned in his own sweat.

The have and the have nots
can often be traced back to
the dids and the did nots.

People that buy
what they don't need
may soon need
what they cannot afford.

An object in possession
seldom retains
the same charm
that it had in the pursuit.

Count your own blessings
let your neighbor
count his.

Do you have too much month left at the end of the money?

Make yourself rich
by making your wants few.

An aim in life
is the only fortune
worth finding.

Money grows on a tree of perserverance.

Some people are as broke
as the
Ten Commandments.

Funny how
a dollar can look so big
when you take it to church
but so small
when you take it to the store.

You will never reach
second base... if you
keep one foot on first.

Where you come from
isn't as important as
where you are going.

We can't run fast enough
to collect the money
which we owe ourselves.

The person who starts out
going nowhere,
generally gets there.

Inflation is being broke in spite of the money in your pocket.

The best time to
buy anything was
last year.

Some people would go
broke if they had to
pay taxes on what they
thought they were worth.

You don't have to be
rich and clever
as long as you hire
people who are.

The most valuable worker
is the one who
lightens the boss's burden.

Good quality is cheap;
it's poor quality
that is expensive.

The best place
for Dublin your money
is in Ireland.

The safest place to
double your money
is to fold it over once
and keep it in your pocket !

If work is so terrific,
how come they have to
pay you to do it?

Work is difficult...
that's why it's called
work.

Nothing is really work
unless you would rather be
doing something else.

Early to bed and early to rise
until you make
enough money to do
otherwise.

A few of us wake up and
find ourselves rich
others wake up and find
they are half an hour late.

It's not economical to
go to bed to save candles
if the result is twins !

The way a young man
spends his evenings
is part of that thin area
between success and failure.

If you try to be rich
before midnight
you might be in jail
before noon.

We don't want to be millionaires
we just want to live like them.

Time is better spent trying
to *solve* problems rather
than going around them.

The middle of the road
is where the white line is,
and that's the worst place
to drive !

I'd rather be laughing on a bicycle than crying in a limousine.

Try to save your money;
who knows ... maybe it will
become valuable again

If you don't want to work, you
have to earn enough money
so you won't have to !

Most people like hard work
particularly
when they are paying
for it to be done.

People who do things
without being told
are the most appreciated.

It's not what you
pay a person
but what it costs you that
counts.

Bankruptcy is when you plan
on early retirement but
your company beats you to it.

Business without advertising
is like winking at a girl
in the dark.
You know what you are doing
but nobody else does.

When business is good
it pays to advertise,
when it's bad
you have to !

Anyone can cut prices but it takes brains to make a better product.

Money never starts an idea
it's the idea
that starts the money.

You can't afford to
waste time when you're
making money.

Time is money, especially overtime.

Luck is what happens when preparation meets opportunity.

It takes twenty years
to make
an overnight success.

It's a proven fact that money
is better than poverty
if only for financial reasons.

To acquire wealth is difficult
but to spend it wisely
is most difficult of all.

Some people think a home is only good to borrow on !

The time to fix the roof is when the sun is shining.

Be kind to people
on the way up,
you may see them
on the way down.

When nobody around you
seems to measure up,
it's time to check
your yardstick.

Money is relative...
the more money that rolls in
the more the relatives.

Money isn't everything
but it sure keeps you
in touch with
your children.

If the check is in the mail,
it is surely made out to
someone else.

Worry is the interest paid
on trouble
before it starts.

There is only one problem
buying on credit...
when you finally own it
you are sick of it.

Beware of the person who has nothing to lose.

Sometimes the best
investment you ever made
is the one you didn't make.

If you don't have it
in the head
you've got to have it in the
pocket book.

One of the hardest things
to teach our children
about money matters
is that it does.

The definition of a living wage depends on whether you are getting it or giving it !

The stock market
is strange in that
you can lose your
life's savings in something
called "securities".

When a stock broker
says it's "bridge night"
you wonder whether he
means playing cards or
jumping !

You're in trouble when your
take home pay
can't survive the trip.

The busy worker is a
happy worker until he finds
out the lazy worker
earns more.

It is better to have
one person working with you
than having three people
working for you.

It is a privilege to pay taxes
but the way they keep going
we may have to give up
the privilege !

There's no such thing as
a sure thing ... that's why
we call it gambling.

Financial success
is how high you bounce
after you have hit bottom.

Economists
not only can't agreee
on the answer, they
can't agree on the problem.

A consultant is a man
who knows 136 ways
to make love but
doesn't know any women.

Some people
stay awake nights trying to
figure out how to become
wealthy... now if they
would only stay awake days.

You can't become rich
if you drop the ball
and complain
about how the ball bounces.

Your most valuable asset
is to have a
good reputation.

You can't build a reputation with what you're going to do.

When you bad mouth the
company you work for
you are actually
bad mouthing yourself.

Don't bad mouth the rich
you'll never get a job from a
a poor person.

Money remains the same it's merely the pockets that change.

There is no future
in any job
only in the person
who holds the job.

Your interest should be in
your future
you're going to spend
the rest of your life there.

The person who says
"it can't be done"
is liable to be interrupted
by someone doing it.

Don't be afraid
of opposition...
remember a kite
rises against the wind.

Either lead, follow
or
get out of the way.

When we are not
fighting over money
we get along just fine.

Success is
getting what you want...
Happiness is wanting
what you get.

Success is
the knack of seeing things
as they are, then doing them
as they ought to be done.

Going bankrupt is a
legal procedure in which you
put your money
in your pants pocket and
give your coat to the creditors.

No one's credit
is as good as their
money.

Beware of the borrower
who says he will be
eternally indebted to you...
he might just do that !

A bad day fishing
still beats
a good day at work.

It takes more and more
money to support the
government
in the manner to which it
has become accustomed.

A reminder for everyone
spending money like there's
no tomorrow
...there is a tomorrow !

If you want something
to last forever...
take out a mortgage.

An entrepreneur
labors sixteen hours a day
to avoid working
for someone else
for eight hours a day.

You know you've made it
when you don't have to
look at your balance before
writing a check.

A status symbol is
anything you couldn't afford
but indulged in it anyway.

You can't do business
with an empty wagon,
but don't get it so full
that the horse can't pull it.

The dictionary is the
only place where
success comes before work.

Life is 10%
what you make it
and 90% how you take it.

A dream is a bargain
no matter
what you pay for it.

Yesterday is a canceled check
tomorrow is a promissory note
today is ready cash... use it.

How did a fool
and his money
get together
in the first place?

AVAILABLE COMPANION BOOKS

Whimsical wisdom in a collection of delightful quotes to
make you think, chuckle, self-motivate & lift your spirits.

ISBN 0-9635176-0-0

ISBN 0-9635176-3-5

ISBN 0-9635176-4-3

ISBN 0-9635176-1-9

ISBN 0-9635176-7-8

ISBN 0-9635176-8-6

ORDER ADDITIONAL BOOKS AS GIFTS

KITTY LITTERATURE
ISBN # 0-9635176-1-9

Qty_____ @ 6.95 Each _____

MOTHERHOOD
is not for Wimps
ISBN # 0-9635176-7-8

Qty_____ @ 6.95 Each _____

**HOW DOES YOUR
GARDEN GROW?**
ISBN # 0-9635176-8-6

Qty_____ @ 6.95 Each _____

MONEY
Now You Have It. Now You Don't.
ISBN # 0-9635176-4-3

Qty_____ @ 6.95 Each _____

THE ROAD TO SUCCESS
Is Always Under Construction
ISBN # 0-9635176-0-0

Qty_____ @ 6.95 Each _____

ACHIEVE YOUR DREAMS
ISBN # 0-9635176-3-5

Qty_____ @ 6.95 Each _____

Add 2.00 for shipping for 1st book, 50¢ ea. thereafter
WA State residents only: add applicable sales tax

Total _____

Send check with order to:

Walrus Productions
4805 N.E. 106th St
Seattle, WA 98125
(206) 364-4365

Name _____

Address _____

City _____

State / Zip _____

These books may be ordered through your local book store.